Choosing a Career as a Model

Modeling is not a career for the lazy. Despite a certain amount of glamour involved in their profession, models have to work very hard.

Choosing a Career as a Model

Cheryl L. Tobey

The Rosen Publishing Group, Inc.
New York

To my father, Frank L. Tobey, Jr.,
who has always been the best kind of model

Published in 2001 by The Rosen Publishing Group, Inc.
29 East 21st Street, New York, NY 10010

Copyright © 2001 by The Rosen Publishing Group, Inc.

First Edition

All rights reserved. No part of this book may be reproduced in any form without permission in writing from the publisher, except by a reviewer.

Library of Congress Cataloging-in-Publication Data

Tobey, Cheryl L.
    Choosing a career as a model / Cheryl L. Tobey
          p.   cm.—(World of work)
Includes bibliographical references and index.
    ISBN 0-8239-3243-5
    1. Models (Persons)—Vocational guidance   [1. Models (Persons)—Vocational guidance. 2. Vocational Guidance.] I. Title. II. Series: World of work (New York, N.Y.)
    HD8039.M77 T63   2000
    746.9'2'02373—dc21

                                                    00-010219

Manufactured in the United States of America

Contents

Introduction

If you've picked up this book, chances are you are wondering what it would be like to be a professional model. Maybe friends or family members have told you that you should model. Perhaps a teacher or guidance counselor has suggested it. Or maybe you've been a fan of fashion for a long time, spending your allowance on *Vogue* and watching MTV's *House of Style*.

What do you think of when you hear the word "model"? You probably picture supermodels like Kate Moss strutting down the runway in designer clothes, or Tyra Banks looking glamorous in the Victoria's Secret catalog. These models are at the top of their field, and it takes a lot of commitment to get there. Most people think that models become successful overnight, or that they spend all their time going to exciting parties or exotic locations. Although there can be a certain amount of glamour involved, models have to work very hard, often putting in long hours and running from one appointment to the next. It is not a career for the lazy.

If you are a hard worker, confident in front of other people, and find the fashion scene appealing, you may be suited for a career as a model.

There are many different kinds of modeling. Fashion modeling has strict physical requirements for height and body type. These are the tall, thin models that appear in fashion magazines and in televised fashion shows. Commercial and specialty modeling, however, allow for a much wider range of looks and sizes. An important thing to remember is that the fashion market is constantly changing. Fifteen years ago, blond-haired, blue-eyed Christie Brinkley was the ideal. Today models with ethnic backgrounds have many more opportunities— although there is still a long way to go.

If you are interested in pursuing a career as a model, you can start preparing yourself right now. Besides reading books and magazines on fashion, take as many business and math courses in high school as you can. After all, modeling is a business. To market themselves, models must be aware of how the fashion industry works. Models also have to negotiate their own contracts. Without solid math skills, it is difficult to judge a favorable contract from a poor one. And instead of daydreaming in French class about appearing in a Paris fashion show, try to learn the language. One of the more exciting aspects of modeling is international travel, and the more languages you know, the better. Physical education and nutrition courses are especially important, since maintaining a healthy diet combined with exercise is one of a model's key responsibilities. In addition, theater and dance classes can build confidence as well as speech and movement skills. You might even want to try a photography course to see what it's like on the other side of the camera.

Math, business, and foreign language skills can be valuable for an aspiring model, so don't neglect your education.

No matter what, don't even think about dropping out of high school to try modeling full-time! Agencies recommend that young models start out working part-time while they are still in school. You can gain valuable experience by modeling after school and on weekends. If your career begins to take off and you need to travel away from home, you can do this over your spring break or summer vacation. Once you graduate, moving to another city to model full-time is an option, but it is not the only one. Some people model and attend college at the same time. Others model full-time for a while and use their earnings to put themselves through college afterward. Remember that along with the perks of a successful modeling career—money, travel, and excitement—come certain realities. For many people, a modeling career may not last more than a few years. For this reason, completing your education is a must.

Tonya was fifteen and a high school sophomore. At five foot nine, she stood at least four inches taller than most of her friends. Tonya participated in track at school and played tennis in the summer. Her friends were always saying that she should try modeling, but Tonya wasn't so sure. Even though she enjoyed flipping through fashion magazines and always tried to look her best, she couldn't exactly see herself posing in flashy outfits or going to trendy parties.

Tonya was more practical and down-to-earth. She was good at math and public speaking and wanted to find a well-paying job someday so that she could afford to travel. She had lived in New Jersey her whole life and was eager to see the rest of the world.

Questions to Ask Yourself

Although modeling is not easy to break into, for the right person it can offer many rewards. 1) Do you find the fashion scene appealing? 2) Are you a hard worker? 3) Are you confident in front of other people?

Starting Out

*A*t the end of the school year, Tonya met with her guidance counselor, Ms. Goldstein. Tonya's mother had told her that she might not have the money to pay for her to go to college. Tonya explained this to Ms. Goldstein, who asked her what her interests were.

Tonya replied that she liked math, public speaking, and sports, and that she wanted to travel. Then she laughed and said that her friends were always saying that she should model.

"Why not?" said Ms. Goldstein. "There was a girl here several years ago who started modeling for fashion shows at the mall. She eventually made enough money to put herself through college." She looked at Tonya. "It's not a bad idea."

Ms. Goldstein gave Tonya the phone number of a local modeling agency. "Just give it a try," she suggested. "You won't have lost anything if it doesn't work out."

It took Tonya two weeks to get up the nerve to call the agency. When she finally did, the man she spoke to was pleasant and direct. He told her to send in a few photographs of herself.

"Do I have to get a professional photographer?" asked Tonya.

"No, not at all," said the man. "Just get your mom or dad to take some snapshots."

Tonya told her mother about her meeting with Ms. Goldstein and her conversation with the man at the modeling agency. Her mother was skeptical, but agreed to take a few pictures of Tonya. Two weeks later, Tonya received a phone call. Someone at the agency wanted to meet with her!

Flawless Photos

One of the most common mistakes that aspiring models make is paying a "professional" photographer for photos. Remember, anyone can claim to be a professional. Many photographers charge high prices for low-quality photographs. All an agency needs is a few snapshots. If they are interested in you, they will have their own photographers work with you to put together a portfolio.

Have a parent or friend take your pictures. You will need two head shots and one body shot. The head shots should include your neck and shoulders. You should be smiling in one and have a relaxed expression in the other. Keep your

You should supply a modeling agency with two head shots. Rather than paying a photographer, have a friend or parent take your pictures.

hairstyle simple and do not wear too much makeup. For the body shot, wear a bathing suit so that the agency can get an idea of your body type and proportions. Either a one- or two-piece suit is fine, but keep it conservative. Wear a solid color, and save the bold patterns and overly revealing styles for the beach. You can also submit a casual shot of yourself in a fun environment or doing a favorite activity. The purpose of this photo is to show your personality.

The best setting for your photos is either outside in natural light or indoors against a pale background. If you have them taken outdoors, do it in the early morning or early evening for the most flattering natural light. Be careful not to submit photos that are overexposed or under-exposed. Include your name and phone number on the back of each one. Once you have three or four good pictures of yourself, you're ready to contact the agencies.

Approaching Modeling Agencies

To pursue a career in modeling, you need a good agency. There are many different ways to find an agent. You can contact smaller agencies, those in major cities such as Chicago or Los Angeles, or agencies in New York—the capital of modeling in the United States. (See the For More Information section at the back of this book for a list of major agencies.) Find out if those in your area have open calls. An open call is a specific time an agency meets with aspiring models. If so, you will be asked to bring your snapshots and a statistics card. This is an index card containing your name, address, phone number, age, height, weight, hair

A casual photo of yourself can give a modeling agency an idea of your personality.

15

and eye colors, special talents, and measurements. The measurements you will need to supply are your chest, waist, and hips.

Open calls frequently have specific age and height requirements, which you may not fit. Also, some agencies do not hold open calls. If this is the case, write a cover letter and mail it in with your snapshots. The letter should contain the same information as a statistics card and should politely ask the agency if they are interested in you or if they have any helpful suggestions. If the agency is interested, they will contact you and ask you to come in for an interview.

Another way to be seen by agency representatives is through model searches and conventions. Model searches are contests in which the winners receive modeling contracts or appear in magazines or advertisements. Some are sponsored by one particular agency, company, or magazine. These searches usually have a very low entrance fee. Others have representatives from many different agencies and may charge several hundred dollars. Conventions, too, can be expensive. These last several days and take place at hotels in major cities. Participants may have the chance to work with hairstylists and makeup artists, walk down the runway, and meet with agents.

In general, if you live near a large city, it is best to approach major agencies directly. If you live in a smaller town, contact local agencies and consider entering model searches with low entrance fees. (For a list of affordable model searches, see the For More Information section at the back of this book.)

Face-to-Face

Whether you are attending an open call, going into an agency for an interview, or entering a model search, you should follow a few basic rules. Keep in mind the way you should appear in your photographs: simple, neat, and natural. Dress in comfortable, form-fitting clothing that is not too revealing. Jeans, pants, T-shirts, and tops are fine. Wear your hair in a simple style, and keep makeup light.

You may be asked to walk so that the agents can see how you move. They may also ask you questions about your school, interests, or plans for the future to get an idea of your personality. It is best to be outgoing and cooperative. Try to make good eye contact and avoid "yes" and "no" answers. Remember, this is a job interview like any other.

If an agent is interested in you immediately, he or she will arrange for you to meet with photographers and other people at the agency. Sometimes an agent may think that an aspiring model has potential but is not quite ready. The person may be asked to attend a model search or to gain some local experience and then reapply. The agent may give advice or suggest areas of improvement. If the advice makes sense to you, follow it. However, be wary of agencies that suggest cosmetic surgery or excessive weight loss

Do not be discouraged if things don't work out after a few open calls or after you've sent out a couple of batches of photos. Most agencies are going for a particular look, and just because you don't fit one agency's image doesn't mean that another one won't want you. If, however, you have tried numerous agencies and model searches without any positive feedback, it may be wise to think about other career choices. There are many exciting careers within the fields of fashion, acting, advertising, and television for which you may be better suited.

A Word of Warning

Before you go into an agency or enter a model search or convention, it is very important to check out its reputation. Unfortunately, the world of modeling is full of dishonest people who cheat aspiring models and their families out of money. A so-called professional photographer may insist that you need an expensive portfolio to show to the agencies. Or a local agency may try to talk you into attending its pricey modeling school.

If you've seen an ad or listing for a modeling agency, search, or convention, there are some ways to check it out:

✔ Call the people who run it and ask which major modeling agencies they are connected to. If they mention names from the For More Information section at the back of this book, it's a good sign.

✔ Ask if you can speak with models they have represented in the past.

✔ Ask what fees are involved. A legitimate agency should not charge you anything to represent you, and expensive searches and conventions may not be worth it.

✔ Call some of the agencies listed at the back of this book and ask if they have heard of the agency or convention.

✔ Get information from people who run local fashion boutiques and hair salons.

✔ Call the Federal Trade Commission (202-326-3650) or your local Better Business Bureau.

Never go alone to meet with an agent or photographer. Have a parent accompany you, or take an older sibling or friend along. The same goes for model searches and conventions. No matter how exciting the opportunity, your safety should always come first.

Questions to Ask Yourself

Beginning a modeling career requires persistence. 1) Do you have a parent or friend who will agree to take your photographs? 2) Can you handle rejection without getting discouraged? 3) Are you willing to spend some time investigating the agencies?

A Foot in the Door

Tonya's mother went with her to the Linda Marino Model and Talent Agency. After showing Tonya and her mother into her office, Ms. Marino said that she had been impressed with Tonya's photographs. She asked Tonya why she wanted to model and what her plans for the future were.

"My friends are always saying that I should model," replied Tonya. "I didn't really take it seriously until I talked to my guidance counselor. Ms. Goldstein gave me your number and said that another girl at school had made a lot of money modeling. I'd like to save for college, and I also want to travel someday."

Ms. Marino explained that her agency had been in business for nine years and that it dealt mostly with catalog and advertising work. She said that some models from her agency had gone on to work for a larger agency in New York. Ms. Marino showed them a copy of Allure *magazine and said that the model on the cover had started with her. She also showed them a thick book full of photographs of various models.*

Tonya's mother asked if they could have the phone numbers of a few models and clients that the agency had worked with. She also asked if they would have to pay any money up front.

Ms. Marino gave Tonya's mother a list of names and said that the agency would receive fees only after Tonya started working. At that point, for every job Tonya completed, 15 percent of Tonya's earnings would go to the agency. "What I would like to do is send Tonya to one of our photographers for a test shoot," she suggested. If the pictures turn out well and we think that Tonya has potential, we'll offer her a contract."

Tonya was very excited, but her mother thanked Ms. Marino and said that they would think it over.

Ms. Marino nodded and said, "I understand. Take all the time you need." She smiled and handed Tonya her business card. "When you're ready to do the test shoot, give me a call."

Shoot for the Stars

A test shoot is a photo session that an agency arranges with one of their photographers. The purpose of a model's first test shoot is to get good photos to put in a portfolio, which will then be shown to clients. Usually the agency will pay for the session, and the cost will be deducted from the model's first paycheck. Test shoots generally cost around $300.

A test shoot with a professional photographer will be very different from having a parent or friend take your picture. A hairstylist and makeup artist will work with you during the shoot, and a variety of different photos will be taken. Some will be close-ups; others will be body shots. You will probably have to project many different moods and emotions. You may also be required to change your clothes or makeup for different shots. The photographer may want you to pose in different settings or with various props.

A good way to prepare for your first test shoot is to practice moving in front of the mirror and trying out various facial expressions. Don't limit your practice time to just posing and trying to look sophisticated. Working in front of the camera is about movement, and versatility is key. It is important for you to go to the shoot with a positive attitude and to be cooperative with the photographer. You should generally be open-minded to the photographer's suggestions. Don't refuse to project a certain mood or to shoot in a specific location because you feel silly. (If, however, a

A hairstylist and a makeup artist prepare a model for a professional photo shoot.

photographer asks you to do something that makes you truly uncomfortable, such as removing clothing or wearing overly revealing attire, it's time to speak up.)

Agencies try to make test shoots as much like the real thing as possible. Think of it not only as a test for yourself, but as a way for you to test out this career. If you dislike moving in front of the camera or working with photographers, hairstylists, and makeup artists, you should rethink modeling as a career choice. After all, this is what you will be doing on a regular basis. If you enjoy the testing process and have fun with the various things you are asked to do, you probably have the right personality for modeling.

Contract Considerations

If your test session goes well and the agency is interested in you, you will be offered a contract. Most contracts last for two years and require a commission of 15 to 20 percent of the model's earnings to be paid to the agency. Contracts are usually exclusive, which means that you may work only with that particular agency within a certain city. The agency may, however, arrange for you to work with other agencies in other cities. The original agency is called the mother agency, and all other agencies must go through the first one in order to book you for work.

Modeling contracts typically state that if the agency cannot market a model successfully or if the model does not perform well, the contract can be broken. It is important that the model also be allowed to end the contract if the agency is not helping his or her career. These statements are known as performance clauses. Many agencies now require models to open a reserve account. The model puts part of his or her earnings into this account to cover expenses paid up front by the agency, such as photographs. This way, the agency is repaid even if the contract is broken.

It is a very good idea to show a contract to a lawyer before you sign it. Tell the agency that you want to think about it for a few days. Be wary of any agency that wants you to sign a contract immediately. Also make sure that the contract does not require you to pay registration fees or to attend a modeling school. And definitely check out the agency with the Better Business Bureau before you sign anything.

Portfolios and Promotion

After the test shoot, the agency chooses which photos to include in the model's portfolio. Models may offer suggestions, but the final decision is up to the agency. Several copies of the portfolio are made, one for the model to bring to appointments and a few to be sent out to clients. Once the model begins working regularly, the test shots will be replaced with tear sheets. These are pictures that have appeared in magazines or other publications.

The agency will also put together the model's composite card. This is a small card that contains several photos along with the model's name and measurements. Composite cards are used by clients for easy reference to particular models. Models carry them to appointments along with their portfolio. Agencies also send clients promotional books and agency head sheets, which contain photos of all the models they represent. Models are required to pay for composites and for their share of the costs of other promotional materials. The money is generally deducted from their paychecks once they begin working.

Let's Go!

Once your portfolio and promotional materials are ready, your agency will start sending you on go-sees. A go-see is a brief job interview with a photographer, agent, editor, client, advertising executive, or anyone else in the position of hiring you. You must bring your portfolio and composite cards to go-sees. The person you are meeting with may ask you to walk or to try on clothing. He or she may also take a snapshot of you.

It is extremely important to arrive on time to a go-see. You should present yourself in a similar way to when you had your first agency appointment. Your hair, makeup, and clothing should be simple and neat. Because there will be many models competing for the job, your personality may decide if you are the one they'll choose. If you are asked questions about your family or school, be friendly and outgoing. You want to project an attitude of confidence, maturity, and enthusiasm. If you are too shy and your personality doesn't come through, the person doing the hiring may figure that you won't project for the camera.

The more go-sees you do, the better you will become. It frequently takes a new model quite a few of these interviews before he or she is offered work. Try not to become discouraged when facing rejection; just take it one step at a time. Eventually you will land your first job, and then you can truly call yourself a model.

Questions to Ask Yourself

Once you have your foot in the agency door, you're on your way. 1) Do you think that a test shoot sounds like a positive experience? 2) Do you or your family know a lawyer who could advise you on your modeling contract? 3) Do you have an outgoing personality?

Fashion Modeling

When most people hear the word "model," they think of supermodels like Cindy Crawford or Mark Vanderloo. These are the high-profile fashion models everyone knows from television and magazines. You see them on the catwalks, in editorial fashion spreads, and in advertisements for cosmetics and designer clothes. You may also see them in movies or hosting television shows. Supermodels are fashion models who are at the top of their field.

If you go into modeling with the hope of becoming a supermodel, you need to be realistic. Most models do not achieve supermodel status; this takes a very rare combination of physical attributes, personality traits, connections, and luck. This doesn't mean that you cannot become a fashion model, however. For those who possess the right qualifications, many opportunities exist within the realm of fashion modeling.

Not everyone can be a supermodel like Mark Vanderloo, but there are plenty of opportunities in the field of modeling.

The Look

More than any other type, fashion models are held to the strictest physical requirements in the business. Although there are occasional exceptions, most female fashion models are between 5'8" and 6' tall and wear a dress size 6 to 8. Although models must be slender and fit, proportions and body type are just as important. The ideal measurements for female fashion models are 34-24-34. It is also best to have long legs, since this makes the model appear even taller. Male models are usually between 6' and 6'2" and wear a suit size 40 to 42. For men, the preferred measurements are a 38- to 40-inch chest and 32 to 34 for both waist and inseam. Male models are generally slim and muscular.

For both men and women, healthy skin, hair, and teeth are essential. A minor breakout can be covered up, but the kind of skin that looks best in photographs is free from pimples, scars, lines, and dark circles. Small pores are also a plus. Hair should be in good condition without split ends. A more natural look is preferable to hair that is overly styled or processed. Straight, white teeth are best, and don't worry if you have braces. It is better to straighten your teeth at a younger age so that the braces will come off by the time your modeling career gets going. For more information on keeping your body, skin, and hair healthy, see chapter 5.

For female fashion models especially, certain other physical attributes can be an advantage. Agents often look for women with long necks, full lips, high cheekbones, wide-set eyes, and

Symmetrical facial features are a desirable trait for female fashion models.

symmetrical facial features. Again, this is because these types of faces tend to photograph well.

Don't despair if you don't have all of these physical traits. For every "rule" in fashion modeling, there is at least one exception. Kate Moss is shorter than the typical fashion model, for example. And some of today's male models are more wiry than muscular. Even if you differ significantly from the standard physical requirements for fashion modeling, you may find opportunities within commercial and specialty modeling, which are discussed in chapter 4.

Editorial Print

For the fashion model, editorial work, also called editorial print, is the most prestigious. When you look through the fashion spreads in magazines like *Vogue* and *Elle*, you are seeing editorial models. It is these magazines that establish trends and determine what is in style. Editorial is known for being creative and allowing the most freedom for the models. For this type of work, the model must be able to move well and project different emotions for the camera. It is very different from catalog modeling, which usually features static poses and models with a more mainstream look.

Although editorial work pays the lowest rate, it generally opens the door to other, more lucrative types of modeling. A beginning model who can replace his or her test photos with editorial tear sheets has a good chance of landing runway shows and advertising deals. A model lucky enough to appear on the cover of a high-profile magazine has reached the top. Not only will the model be in great demand, but the amount of money he or she can command will increase drastically.

Most of the editorial work in the United States is in New York City. There is more of this type of modeling in foreign cities such as Paris, Milan, London, Toronto, and Sydney. For this reason, agents often send new models abroad to get editorial experience and tear sheets for their portfolios. Although some editorial work is available in other large cities in the United States, including Chicago and Miami, it is harder to find editorial in smaller markets. If you live in a small city or town, you may have to travel to do this type of modeling. It is best to discuss this with your agent and your family.

Editorial print work generally pays around $200 a day. In the world of modeling, this is a very low day rate. It is important to remember, however, that editorial work almost always leads to more opportunities and a higher salary down the road.

Runway

Today there is a big overlap between editorial work and runway modeling. Often a model who has worn a designer's clothing in a fashion magazine is hired to do that designer's runway show. At the same time, since high-profile fashion shows are attended by designers, magazine editors, agents, and photographers, runway models are frequently spotted and offered editorial print work. Because of this overlap, runway modeling is becoming much more prestigious.

The experience of runway modeling is completely different from editorial. A fashion show is a live performance that often includes music, dramatic lighting, and elements of theater. Runway models must attend go-sees, fittings, and rehearsals. Models usually pause several times on the catwalk so that the clothes are shown off to their best advantage. A model who can go down the catwalk with confidence and wear the clothes with a sense of style will be in great demand.

Designer fashion shows typically take place in New York, Paris, and Milan as well as London, Tokyo, and other major cities. Fall collections are usually presented in March, and spring collections in October. During this time, a model may do

A fashion show is a theatrical performance. Runway models who can go down the catwalk with style and confidence are in great demand.

several shows in one day. Local fashion shows in malls, clothing stores, and hair salons also provide opportunities for runway modeling. These shows often do not pay much, but they are a great way to get experience while you are still in school.

The rate of pay for runway modeling in major cities can range from a few hundred dollars per show for an unknown designer to $10,000 for top designers and clients. Keep these figures in mind if your first runway show at the local mall is unpaid.

Fashion Advertising

Fashion models also appear in upscale advertisements for designer clothing, cosmetics, and fragrances. Advertising contracts state how long the ad will run and often prohibit the model from appearing in ads for competing products. These are known as exclusive contracts and usually pay the highest rates. Models featured in television commercials may earn fees called residuals every time the commercial is shown.

The purpose of advertising work is to make the product look appealing to the consumer. Models who want to appear in television commercials generally need to take acting lessons. This helps them project their voice and adjust their facial expressions so their dialogue is believable.

Some very lucky models are offered endorsement deals. This means that they are paid huge amounts of money to represent a particular product for several years, both in advertisements and at business-related events. Most people are familiar with the models who have landed endorsement deals with large cosmetics companies. A model with an endorsement deal cannot represent other products that are thought to be less respectable. Because the image of the company relies on the model, he or she must be professional at all times.

Fashion advertising is most commonly produced in New York, Paris, and Milan. There is also some upscale advertising work in Los Angeles, Chicago, and Miami. Smaller cities have advertising too, but it is usually of a more commercial nature and does not appear nationally. It is, however, a good way to get experience while you are still in school. (For more information on commercial modeling, see chapter 4.)

Advertising work in major cities typically pays between $200 and $250 an hour. In addition, residuals for television commercials can add up to thousands of dollars. Remember, if your dream is to be a Cover Girl spokesmodel, find yourself an agent, take acting classes, and avoid unprofessional behavior!

Questions to Ask Yourself

For people with the right look, fashion modeling can provide many opportunities. 1) Do you have most of the physical requirements necessary to be a fashion model? 2) Do you live in or near a major city? 3) Would you rather see your picture in a magazine, perform in a live show, or speak in front of the camera?

Commercial and Specialty Modeling

If you don't look like Christy Turlington, don't despair. The worlds of commercial and specialty modeling offer many opportunities—both for attractive models who fall short of the physical requirements for fashion modeling, and for people with a more everyday look.

Commercial Modeling

Commercial modeling typically means modeling for catalogs and advertisements. Although fashion modeling and commercial modeling do overlap, catalogs and nonfashion advertisements generally require a look that consumers can relate to. Clothing catalogs feature attractive, healthy-looking models who seem like the girl or guy next door. And there are opportunities in advertising for models who look just like regular people.

There are no specific physical requirements for commercial models, except that they have the look the client wants for its product. J. Crew models project a very different image from those in the

Delia's catalog. A model who is perfect for soap commercials is not necessarily appropriate for shampoo ads.

If you are interested in being a commercial model, call agencies in your area and ask if they handle commercial work. You may be asked to send snapshots. Once you have an agent, he or she will refer you to a photographer to have pictures taken for a composite card and a portfolio or head shot. Then you will be sent on go-sees and auditions with casting directors.

Catalog

Catalog work may not seem as glamorous as appearing in a fashion spread, but it pays well and can provide a steady income. The purpose of catalog modeling is to make the clothes look appealing to the consumer. Models tend to look more mainstream and are shown in common poses so that customers can identify with them. Those models appear in mail-order catalogs and brochures for department stores.

In catalog shoots, the client wants to do as much work as possible within a short amount of time. Bookings may last from one hour to a week, and it is not uncommon to photograph twenty different outfits during one shoot. The model must be able to change clothes quickly and know how to make clothing look its best.

One advantage of catalog modeling is that there are more opportunities in regional markets. In addition to New York, major markets include Chicago, Los Angeles, Miami, Dallas, Atlanta, and

Work for catalog models is available in many regional markets. It pays well and can provide you with a steady income.

Seattle. In smaller cities and towns, catalog work is frequently available through local department stores and boutiques.

Catalog work generally pays around $150 an hour, and top catalog models can make up to $50,000 a day.

Advertising

Advertising work includes modeling for print ads and television commercials. In advertising, the model must have an appropriate look for the product. A model with great skin may appear in beauty ads for skin-care products. There is also a need for more regular-looking types, known as character models. Character models are frequently used in television commercials. A character model may be asked to portray a young professional or a police officer. As in fashion advertising, acting skills are very important.

Although national ads are usually produced in big cities, local advertisements are produced everywhere. In addition to New York, Los Angeles, Chicago, Miami, Toronto, Atlanta, and Dallas, models can find advertising work in almost any regional market. Local newspaper ads, billboards, and TV commercials generally use local models and are a great way to get started.

Advertising work pays very well. Depending on the location and the type of ad, a commercial model can earn between $50 and $250 an hour. Exclusive contracts usually pay the highest rates. Models featured in television commercials may earn residuals every time the commercial is shown, which can add up to thousands of dollars.

Specialty Modeling

Various types of specialty modeling overlap with the world of commercial modeling. Women may work as petite or plus-size models. These models have similar proportions and physical attributes to regular models but wear sizes that are smaller or larger than what is standard for fashion modeling. Petite models can find jobs in advertising, and a lot of catalog work is available for plus-size models. In addition, opportunities exist for both men and women in body parts modeling. Although specialty modeling has its own physical requirements, the same skills are necessary as in regular modeling: the ability to move well, to make products look appealing, and to project emotions.

The best way to get started in specialty modeling is to call agencies in your area and ask if they handle petite, plus-size, or parts models. Larger agencies may have separate divisions for these types of modeling. Some agencies specialize in plus-size models. For any kind of specialty modeling, you will probably need snapshots. Once you are offered an interview, the process is similar to that of regular modeling. If you have potential, you will be sent to a photographer to build a portfolio and composite card.

Good Things Come in Small Packages

Many attractive women are shorter than 5'8" and wear a dress size smaller than 6 to 8. If you fall into this category, you may be able to work as a petite model. Petite models are frequently used in beauty advertisements, which focus on the face. They may appear in both print ads and television commercials. Although rarely used in editorial fashion spreads or major runway shows, they may model for designers' petite collections or for catalogs featuring petite or junior sizes. Since smaller proportions work well for parts modeling, they can also branch out into this area.

Petite models are typically between 5'2" and 5'7" and wear a dress size 2 to 6 petite. Whereas fashion models measure approximately 34-24-34, petite models should measure around 32-22-32. Even though the model's overall size is smaller, her body proportions should be about the same. As in fashion modeling, it is also desirable to have clear skin, healthy hair, good teeth, symmetrical facial features, wide-set eyes, high cheekbones, a long neck, and long legs.

Since most petite modeling is commercial, petites can usually find opportunities in markets with advertising and catalog work. This includes New York, Chicago, Los Angeles, Miami, Atlanta, Seattle, and Toronto. These models can also get jobs in smaller cities with locally produced advertisements and catalogs. Models are paid the standard rates for catalog and advertising work.

Bigger Is Better

Recently there has been an increasing demand for plus-size models because of changes in the fashion industry. Most American women are not nearly as thin as fashion models. In the past, many women have found it difficult to shop for clothes or to relate to the models in magazines and catalogs. At last, designers, clothing manufacturers, and fashion editors are responding to the need for larger sizes, which in turn creates a need for larger models. Plus-size models appear in catalogs, print ads, television commercials, and in editorial print. If you are interested in becoming a plus-size model, this is a great time to enter the business.

Plus-size models are typically 5'8" to 5'11" and wear a dress size 10 to 20. Proportions are similar to those of regular models, with measurements usually from two to eight inches larger for bust, waist, and hips. The same requirements for hair, skin, facial features, and body type are equally

Recently, there has been an increasing demand for plus-size models.

important for plus-size models. As in other types of modeling, confidence and the ability to move well in front of the camera are essential.

Plus-size models can find jobs in regional markets such as Los Angeles, Chicago, Dallas, Atlanta, Seattle, and Toronto. Most of the editorial work for these models is in New York, however. Rates of pay generally conform to those of regular models and vary depending on the type of work.

Parts Models

If you have ever seen a woman's legs on a hosiery package or a man's hands in a TV commercial, you have noticed parts models. These models have a body part—usually hands, legs, or feet—that photographs well and fits a certain look or size. They may be used in advertisements or catalogs. Parts models often appear with regular models or celebrities who have less perfect parts.

To find work, parts models must have flattering snapshots of their hands, legs, feet, or whatever part they wish to model. Hand models need pictures of their hands in different poses; women should have some with nail polish and some without. Foot and leg models must have pictures in which they are barefoot as well as wearing shoes. Women should have some pictures with toenail polish and some with high-heeled shoes. These photos can then be sent out to agencies.

Female hand models should wear a glove size 6 1/2 to 7 1/2 and a ring size 4 1/2 to 5 1/2. Their hands must be well manicured and free from scars, with long, thin fingers. Male hand models wear a glove size 8 1/2 to 10 and may have either elegant or rugged-looking hands. Leg models must have long, toned legs without bruises or scrapes. Foot models need to keep their feet pedicured and free from calluses and blisters.

Parts models can find opportunities just about anywhere advertisements are produced. More work is available in larger cities, however. Rates of pay vary according to the type of job.

Questions to Ask Yourself

Commercial and specialty modeling provide opportunities for those who do not meet the strict requirements of fashion modeling. 1) Which is more important to you in a job: glamour or stability? 2) Do you have a look that most consumers can relate to? 3) Are you appropriate for petite, plus-size, or parts modeling?

Responsibilities
and Risks

*T*onya eventually had her test shoot and was offered a contract. Soon she began modeling after school and on weekends for local catalogs and advertisements. The clients liked Tonya's cooperative attitude and often asked to use her again. Unlike some of the other models, Tonya was never late to photo shoots. Once her hair and makeup were done, she usually did her homework while the photographers were setting up.

One Thursday afternoon, Tonya was alone in the dressing room waiting for a shoot to begin. The door opened, and a very thin blond girl walked in. Tonya looked up from her English book. "Hi," she said. "I'm Tonya."

"I'm Samantha," the girl said softly. "Is this the dressing room for the Sears catalog shoot?"

Tonya nodded. "I don't think they'll be ready to go for about an hour."

"That's okay," said Samantha, putting her bag down in one of the chairs. "Is there a bathroom in here?"

"Yeah, just to your left."

Samantha disappeared into the bathroom for about ten minutes. Tonya went back to her homework but stopped when she heard a gagging sound. A few minutes later, Samantha came out of the bathroom.

"Are you okay?" asked Tonya. "It sounded like you were sick."

Samantha shrugged. "No, I'm fine. I actually feel much better now. My mom took me out for pizza after school, and I was feeling really fat."

Modeling carries with it a lot of responsibility, both to the client and to yourself. Clients want to work with models they can depend on. Part of this means showing up on time with a professional attitude. The other part means taking care of yourself so that you can continue to model successfully. A model who neglects to take care of his or her body, health, and appearance will not stay long in the business. Unfortunately, some models fall prey to dangerous habits that threaten not only their careers but their lives as well. These dangers will be discussed later in this chapter.

It is important for models to keep their skin in good condition.

Hair and Skin Care

If you are interested in modeling, it is important to keep your hair and skin in good condition. Considering all the beauty products that are applied during photo shoots, this is not necessarily easy. Your hair should be washed and conditioned frequently, and you should have it trimmed every month to month and a half. When you're off the job, try not to blow-dry it or use styling products. If your hair is wet, use a comb instead of a brush. And wear a bathing cap in the pool, since chlorine can damage your hair.

As far as skin care goes, models have to find what works for their particular skin type. Washing your face two to three times a day with a mild soap or cleanser is a good place to start. If your skin is oily, an astringent can be helpful; if it is dry, you need to find a good moisturizer. Also try to drink plenty of water, and always wear sunscreen when you spend time outdoors. If you have a lot of trouble with your skin, it can be useful to see a dermatologist.

Diet and Nutrition

Most models have to eat a healthy diet to maintain their ideal weight. This does not mean eating only lettuce leaves or bouncing from one fad diet to the next. A healthy diet allows you to eat a variety of foods in order to receive proper nutrition. In general, you should try to eat mostly lean meats or soy products, whole grains, and plenty of vegetables

Like everyone else, models should eat a variety of foods to receive proper nutrition. Fruits and vegetables are a healthy choice for snacks.

and fruits. Lean meats include fish, chicken, turkey, and lean cuts of beef or pork. Meats should be grilled or baked, not fried. Soy products include tofu and soy "meats." Whole grains include pasta, rice, couscous, and whole-grain breads and cereals.

It is okay to eat more fattening foods in moderation. Let yourself have a treat like french fries or chocolate cake once a week. This way, it won't be so hard to eat well the rest of the time. Although it is best to keep fattening snacks to a minimum, other kinds of snacks can be healthy. Instead of potato chips and ice cream, snack on fruits and vegetables. These foods will provide you with vitamins and minerals instead of fat and calories. If you have questions about nutrition, it is best to speak to your doctor or your agent. He or she may be able to answer your questions or refer you to a dietitian.

Exercise and Rest

Without exercise and plenty of rest, a model cannot keep his or her body in top condition. There are many different ways to exercise. You don't necessarily have to go to the gym or stick to the same kind of workout. Aerobic exercises such as walking, running, dancing, skating, biking, and swimming will burn calories, tone your muscles, and condition your heart. Working out with weights or doing sit-ups and push-ups will also strengthen your muscles. Yoga will keep your body flexible and will reduce stress. The best workout programs involve a combination of activities. You should try to exercise three to four times a week.

Sleep is important for everyone, especially for models. Too much partying will not result in a good photo shoot. Clients need models who look energetic and healthy, not those with dull skin and dark circles. Insufficient sleep also tends to cause a negative attitude rather than a cooperative one. You should get at least eight hours of sleep a night. If it is the night before an important job and you are having trouble falling asleep, try taking a warm bath, listening to soft music, or reading a good book (or all three).

Modeling Dangers

Sometimes models take up dangerous or unhealthy practices in order to deal with pressure or insecurity. A young model who feels that he or she does not measure up physically may try to achieve the right look through plastic surgery or excessive dieting or exercise. Other models abuse alcohol or drugs as a way to fit in or ease their stress. All of these practices are dangerous and can ruin a young model's career.

Plastic Surgery

Because of the strict physical requirements and the level of competition involved, some models go to drastic lengths to achieve their idea of the perfect body or look. Operations such as liposuction, breast enlargement, and calf implants are not new in the modeling world. However, plastic surgery always carries a certain amount of risk, particularly for young people who haven't finished growing. These expensive operations can produce scarring or infection, and the results do not always turn out as expected. If your natural look isn't right for modeling, it is probably best to pursue another career.

Eating Disorders

Some people, such as Samantha in the story at the beginning of this chapter, become so obsessed with controlling their weight that they develop eating disorders. Conditions such as anorexia, bulimia, and exercise addiction will ruin a model's health and can eventually cause death if left untreated. People with anorexia have such a fear of gaining weight that they starve themselves. Bulimics overeat and then try to make up for it by vomiting or taking laxatives. Exercise addiction is similar to bulimia, but the person uses excessive exercise to get rid of the calories. If you think that you have an eating disorder or are developing an unhealthy relationship with food, tell a parent, your family doctor, or your agent right away.

Drugs and Alcohol

Most young people today have been warned about drug and alcohol abuse. These problems exist everywhere and are certainly not specific to the modeling industry. However, young models are exposed to situations in which alcohol and drugs are readily available, perhaps even more so than for the average teenager. Not only may models go to more upscale parties and nightclubs than most teenagers, but they generally have much more money at their disposal. The combination of this party lifestyle, the money, and the daily pressures a young model faces make addiction a very real threat. Models with a responsible attitude limit their partying and avoid abusing alcohol and drugs because they know that their success, health, and happiness are at stake.

Is Modeling for You?

By now, you probably have some idea of whether you are interested in pursuing a career as a model. Although there are many different types of modeling, they all require commitment, persistence, and professionalism. If you have these attributes and feel that you are suited for a career in modeling, go for it! Turn to the For More Information section to get started.

Questions to Ask Yourself

As a model, your primary responsibility is to take care of yourself. 1) Do you try to keep your hair and skin in good condition? 2) Could you maintain a healthy diet on a long-term basis? 3) What forms of exercise do you enjoy?

Glossary

body shot   Photograph that shows a model's entire body, usually in a bathing suit.

composite   Small card that contains a model's name, measurements, and several photos.

editorial print   Modeling work that appears in the fashion pages of magazines.

endorsement deal   Agreement in which a model is paid to represent a particular product for a long period of time.

exclusive contract   Advertising contract that prohibits a model from appearing in ads for competing products.

go-see   Brief job interview for modeling work.

head shot   Photograph that shows a model's face, neck, and shoulders.

mother agency   Original agency with which a model begins his or her career.

open call   Specific time an agency meets with aspiring models.

performance clause   Term in a modeling contract that allows it to be broken if the model or the agency does not perform well.

portfolio　Book of photographs that a model shows to clients.

reserve account　Bank account containing a portion of a model's earnings, used to repay the agency for expenses covered up front.

residuals　Fees paid to models featured in television commercials every time the commercial is shown.

tear sheets　Pictures of a model that have appeared in magazines or other publications.

test shoot　Photo session that an agency arranges for a model with one of their photographers.

W∆W

For More Information

Modeling Agencies In the United States

Aria Model & Talent
  Management
1017 West Washington
  Blvd. Suite 2C
Chicago, IL 60607
(312) 243-9400

Arlene Wilson Model
  Management
887 West Marietta Street
Atlanta, GA 30318
(404) 876-8555

Click Model
  Management
129 West 27th Street
New York, NY 10001
(212) 206-1616

Click Model
  Management
1688 Meridian Avenue
Miami Beach, FL 33139
(305) 674-9900

Elite Model
  Management
111 East 22nd Street
New York, NY 10010
(212) 529-9700

Elite Model
Management
58 West Huron Street
Chicago, IL 60610
(312) 943-3226

Ford Models
142 Greene Street
New York, NY 10012
(212) 966-3565

Ford Models
8826 Burton Way
Beverly Hills, CA 90211
(310) 276-8100

Irene Marie Model
   Management
728 Ocean Drive
Miami Beach, FL 33139
(305) 672-2929

Page Parkes Models Rep
3303 Lee Parkway
Dallas, TX 75219
(214) 526-4434

Seattle Models Guild
1809 Seventh Avenue
Seattle, WA 98101
(206) 622-1406

Wilhelmina Models
300 Park Avenue South
New York, NY 10010
(212) 473-0700

Wilhelmina Models
8383 Wilshire
Boulevard
Beverly Hills, CA 90211
(213) 655-0909

In Canada

Agence Folio Montreal
295 de la Commune
   Ouest
Montreal, QB H2Y 2E1
(514) 288-8080

Elite Model
Management
477 Richmond
   Street West
Toronto, ON M5V 3E7
(416) 369-9995

Ford Models Canada
385 Adelaide
   Street West
Toronto, ON M5V 1S4
(416) 362-9208

Model Searches

Elite Model Look
111 East 22nd Street
New York, NY 10010
(212) 529-9700

Ford Supermodel
  of the World
142 Greene Street
New York, NY 10012
(212) 966-3565

Seventeen Magazine
850 Third Avenue,
  9th Floor
New York, NY 10022
(212) 407-9700

Wilhelmina Mode
  Model Search
(for plus-size models)
300 Park Avenue South
New York, NY 10010
(212) 473-0700

Web Sites

www.fordmodels.com
Official Web site of the
Ford modeling agency

www.howtomodel.com
Information on
commercial modeling

www.models
international.com
Advice for aspiring
models

www.supermodel.com
Developed by Niki
Taylor and her mother,
this site contains
information on the
Model Search
America contest.

www.wilhelmina.com
Official Web site of
Wilhelmina Models

WΦW

For Further Reading

Boyd, Marie Anderson. *Model: The Complete Guide for Men and Women*. Westport, CT: Peter Glenn Publications, 1997.

Esch, Natasha, and C.L. Walker. *The Wilhelmina Guide to Modeling*. New York: Simon & Schuster, 1996.

Fried, Stephen. *Thing of Beauty: The Tragedy of Supermodel Gia*. New York: Pocket Books, 1994.

Gearhart, Susan Wood. *Opportunities in Modeling Careers*. Lincolnwood, IL: VGM Career Horizons, 1999.

Gross, Michael. *Model: The Ugly Business of Beautiful Women*. New York: William Morrow & Company, 1995.

Peter Glenn staff. *International Directory of Model & Talent Agencies & Schools*. New York: Peter Glenn Publications, 1999.

Rose, Yvonne, and Tony Rose. *Is Modeling for You? The Handbook and Guide for the Young Aspiring Black Model*. Phoenix, AZ: Amber Books, 1997.

Rubinstein, Donna, and Jennifer Kingson Bloom. *The Modeling Life.* New York: Penguin Putnam Inc., 1998.

Sommers, Annie Leah. *Everything You Need to Know About Looking and Feeling Your Best.* New York: Rosen Publishing Group, 1999.

Williams, Roshumba, and Anne Marie O'Connor. *The Complete Idiot's Guide to Being a Model.* New York: Alpha Books, 1999.

Index

About the Author

Cheryl L. Tobey is an editor and freelance writer based in Chicago. Her articles have appeared in the *Chicago Tribune* and the *Performing Arts Journal*. She is currently working on a series of dance books for young adults.

Photo Credits

Cover © Michael Paras/International Stock; p. 2 © James Davis/International Stock; p. 7 © Ira Fox; p. 9 © Telegraph Colour Library; p. 14 © Michael Paras/International Stock; p. 15, 34, 43 © Corbis; p. 23 © The Everett Collection; p. 29 © The Everett Collection; p. 31 © Nancy Ney/FPG; p. 39 © Flip Chalfant/Image Bank; p. 48 © Larry Gatz/Image Bank; p. 50 © Ken Ross/Image Bank.

Series Design

Geri Giordano

Layout

Laura Murawski